CW01573135

REMAINS

Remains

A Collection of Poems

By

Peter Southall

First published in 2014 on behalf of the author by
Scotforth Books (www.scotforthbooks.com)
ISBN 978-1-909817-09-8
Typesetting and design by Carnegie Publishing, Lancaster.
Printed in the UK by PODW

For Mum and Dad

Introduction

Remains: 1) things that remain or are left. 2) historical or archaeological relics. 3) a person's body after death. (OED – Oxford University Press)

If humans living 1,000 years from now were to find the remnants of 21st century life, what would they make of us? If they found the statue of Karl Marx in Highgate Cemetery, would they think he was once our leader? When changes occur, something or someone is always left behind. Death leaves behind grief, confusion and a sometimes seemingly endless void for loved ones; the pulling down of buildings and communities in the name of progress can leave only time and memories. Poetry can be the remains (or product) of days and weeks of contemplation and frustration. When societies change, people and communities can be left behind as ruthless political agendas accelerate countries in directions that are bereft of kindness, compassion and love. As the most affluent in societies become even richer, the most vulnerable become poorer in terms of income, health and time, making life a daily battle of survival. Recent cuts to our benefits system have ensured that millions of people are finding it impossible to afford even the basic essentials of life.

The poem Unidentified Male looks at a tragic case of homelessness through the eyes of someone who blames himself for losing sight of a friend when he needed help. The poem Arcade Murder challenges the drone attacks currently killing thousands of innocent people across the world, whilst poems such as Blink and Meltdown attempt to confront and satirise specific injustices and inequalities contained within societies, such as monarchy systems and certain attitudes towards the global financial collapse.

Some of the poems in this collection attempt to address how sometimes it is possible for all of us to feel left behind as life accelerates into the distance and everything seems beyond control. As a Christian, I believe that we should live together in faith, humility and gentleness, bearing one another's burdens and taking care not to be consumed by greed or ambition.

The most influential poet in my life has been Christina Rossetti. I still remember the first time I read her debut collection Goblin Market and Other Poems, and the immediate affinity I felt with the poet. The sensuality, clarity of language and emotional complexity of Rossetti's poems still make a visceral impact whenever I read them. The subject matter of the poems are still just as relevant today as they were when they were first written. For example, Goblin Market could have been written in response to the banking outrages when Lizzie warns Laura:

"We must not look at Goblin men,
We must not buy their fruits
Who know upon what soil they fed
Their thirsty hungry roots"

I believe that poetry, whatever its message, should be enjoyed by the reader. I hope you enjoy the collection.

Kindness,

Peter Southall

Contents

Demolition

Now they are pulling the old town down,
Avenue by avenue, home by home.
Rooms with stories of their own are reduced
In seconds to heaps of beams and boulders –
The usual wreckage of surrender,
Or brazen barricades of defiance.
I watch white dust vanish in the high wind
And imagine the remains of Coventry.

I did not imagine I would outlive
My town, or at least the everyday town
I knew – it did not cross my naïve mind.
A weather tilted fence is protecting
These freshly leveled courtyards of progress,
As restless rooms are struck and gouged open,
A detached butchering of a rotting
Corpse not ready to be given up.

A clumsy demolition ball connects
And airbrushes another drained household,
I think of lives never lived and the new
Ones left to incubate in these ruins –
Do flowers ever rise from a wasteland?
Still, there is much peace amongst this labour,
Nods of approval from the passers-by
Just grateful perhaps for activity?

A child is following the bulldozer's
Craning neck, fermenting her resentment,
Searching for memories in the rubble
As she clings to the fence, breathing the dust
Drifting from the rising mountains of brick –
But her inconvenient community
Has been marched and led to the promised land
Of legacy and regeneration.

Funfair

I remember worrying about mud,
That fatty clay caking and spattering
The pressed creases of my Sunday best.
I stretched on tiptoe to slip my last coin
Into the cratered hand of the funfair-man.

I would be patient for my cold scolding,
Rules were laws and wash days were Wednesdays,
But I felt a delicious abandon
That last came with the generous helping
Of unloved snow that shut the school in May.

The tents flapped and cracked like a crazed stingray,
I slipped from Dad's hand and held the rifle
In my tiny unaccustomed fingers.
There were no rough edges, just cold-blooded iron
And glassy wood that didn't smell of death.

I scrunched the butt against my shoulder
And was a brave red-coat at Raulk's Drift,
A hero of the undefendable.
I would never suffer the stench of school
Again, as I aimed a braced for the kick.

The Fight

Foaming dogs strain at chains, sun-mad
And rib-starved, marching under leaden skies,
Dragging their murmuring, slavering pack
Towards the alleyway battlefield.

Birds have rested on rooftops, patient
For entertainment, silent spectators
Of brutal theatre, unreliable
Witnesses singing remarkable tales.

The sleight has been festering all night
In both dens, where cracks of knuckle and bone
Will compete with church bells at Evensong,
As avenues of twitching veils swish shut.

Kickabouts have scattered home to the beat
Of pounding fists and absent-minded
Cracks of bicycle chains whipped at walls;
The armies charge like a bitter winter.

Neither side has badge or uniform
To betray their squandered allegiance,
Their legs and arms are lashed in blind anger
In a clumsy maul full of foolish hate.

Until, like colliding atoms, the crowd
Scatters to the melody of sirens
And belting rain that could never rinse,
The rage oozing along these pavement cracks.

Match Day

The Watchers wind their paths down sizzling streets,
The army is almost at the Red gate
Where strangers embrace, where fathers sing Red
Songs and sons cling tightly to freezing hands.

The sweep up white breathless steps reveals
Our loud undulating coliseum
Where battlelines are rolled and formations
Assemble to the din of practiced prayers.

Those Red men, at potency's summit like
Autumn's ripe fruit, shimmy their bruised limbs through
The enemy's confused ranks, thrusting their sabre
Through vacant uncomprehending sentries.

Misshapen boulders erupt, their scalding
Lava bursting from the crumbling crust,
Swilled with a steaming primordial gloup;
Sweet Ambrosia from the Red kitchen!

A murmur grows from grains within the field;
The Watchers swell, a soaring melody
Expands slowly like a quickening pulse,
This battle hymn asks for no forgiveness!

The Watchers wind their paths down closing streets,
Dispatches mentioned, formations redrawn,
The carcass of battle is picked until,
They wind their way down sizzling streets again.

Welcome To Sheffield

The shale and sidings are a snug fit with
Fresh graffiti under open windows,
As the muffled snarl of the tired engine
Reminds us the city of steel is close.

Bust rivers choke the besieged fields
That seem overwhelmed with the attention
From saints and amateur meddlers –
Perhaps welcoming anonymity?

Battleship clouds assemble above
Clumps of trees huddled like bomb-broken soldiers,
A last natural resistance against
The creaking spread of the iron tumour.

The outer rim of this city seems to
Wear the scars of a lost argument,
As we pause against the buzzing platform –
The door to real lives and activity.

The engine gently pulls away our carriage
Of strangers who will never meet,
Or know the lives impounded behind,
The upturned wagons of suburban streets.

Would Like To Meet

They cordoned off the scene of crime
With flimsy tape of white and red,
The village bells began to chime
As they draped poor Lizzie's head.

A torch was shone into dry eyes
As dark as her mud-matted hair,
She stared in peace towards the sky,
Perhaps for one unfinished prayer.

The few around who knew her life
Remarked upon her friendly ways,
And asked how could he find the knife
That put an end to Lizzie's days.

The gossip spread through press and wire,
Of jealous lover's pushed away
Or the unrequited desire
Perhaps, of a hidden fiancé.

But only Lizzie knew for sure,
How her solitary fingers clicked
In search of a virtual cure;
How could she let herself be tricked!?

The page had urged to chat a while
Before a contact is arranged,
But Lizzie with her misplaced guile
Decided that her life must change.

The time to meet soon came around
As Lizzie gazed upon herself,
And smiled upon the site she found,
No danger now of second's shelf!

As dreams and plans became as one,
The murky clouds foretold the night,
At last her new life had begun
As Lizzie skipped towards her knight.

No-one could guess the final blaze
Of innocent thought, as pure as pearl,
That raced across poor Lizzie's gaze,
As the blade fell upon this girl.

Her cries soon weakened to echoes,
In the silence of a night
Broken by the rising tempo
Of vigour in the swelling light.

The nation vented its outrage,
Its shock, disgust – its disbelief,
Until the red-tops turned the page
In favour of a Square Mile thief!

Poor Lizzie now rests below the bed
Of yellow petals yet unseen,
The shared crime is her short life's thread
Will never advance beyond thirteen.

The Liberation of Blue

Its clever guises layered each new day,
Everywhere but forever out of reach,
That colour with a multitude of moods
We should experience, not calculate.
I reserved one of its abundant shades
For the memory of a childhood sketch,
When I was ignorant of its power
And how it petrified authority.

Banished by bishops, embraced by Titian,
Brilliance hunted as a fugitive,
St. Peter achieved immortality
Soaked in the juices of its ultramarine,
Just like a perfectly forged piece of sky.
I can imagine the excitement when
Merchants first unveiled Lapis Lazuli,
Unleashing that glittering gunpowder.

Exalted through the pen of Novalis,
Beguiling the young Von Ofterdingen,
Whose flower was an impossible quest;
Its burn illuminated manuscripts,
Igniting its silent revolution
Into long eliminated vigour,
Ever censored by an ordained ignorance –
But gifting us its electric spectrum.

Alexander

Each morning from his oak veneered throne,
He surveys his claret-red velvet realm;
Walls of ammunition-loaded optics,
Lengthening shadows along the green baize.

He will reign over tired philosophers,
The jesters and the shy professionals,
Who stray inside his kingdom to nod
To the Father of their Marshalsea.

The slow drift builds to a bustle by noon,
As subjects jostle to be ennobled,
And spin the same old sacrilegious tales
Given fresh twists from wasted memories.

Darkness at last surrounds his dominion;
The music stops, the chairs are swept away
And the court disperses at the third chime,
As the sands of his empire run dry.

He curses his fleeting abdication
When he must morph into a mortal man,
As he shuffles down familiar streets and weeps,
For his only kingdom still to conquer.

The Colour of God

Its ubiquity was lost on me,
Until Mam explained the history
Of the piece I knew I must not lose.
I had seen the colour before
Of course, on those serious
Programs I was allowed to glimpse,
Before the next chapter of the Five
Find Outers coasted me to the safety
Of a perfect world I cannot remember.

I thought it did not exist
In my world, until I found it
On ears and fingers, through noses and lips;
Like bubbles from the eruption
Of the first crack of lemonade
It seemed to be everywhere at once –
Thick as cuts of fishermen's rope
Wrapped in a glossy grout, show-offs
Elbowing to the front of open shirts.

I discovered that most ancient
Civilizations in my books
Saved the best burials for dwarfs,
The skilled special ones who fashioned
Their objects of envy, the subjects
Of wars and age-long attritional
Struggles to extinction – the prizes
Never died, just shifted continents
Until the next dictator's appetite.

Kings no longer begin their next life
Surrounded by its glistening
Reassurance, instead, it lays
Buried in the bowels of Threadneedle
And traded across telephone wires,
Hoarded by those who drool over nothing
But its demand, and not how its colour
Can gently heal and caress a canvass
By a certain candlelight.

Unidentified Male

He and I would collide when I returned
Along our teeming, untouched avenue
In that corner of our forgotten town.
He held a faith, he participated
And gladly gave his cut to Caesar,
He shaved and weeded and tended estates
Where the young were backhanded to forget;
But I remember the name he gave me.

The strike came suddenly, like the spinning
Of impossible options after the
Creeping submission of cells.
Everything turned black; the van, the suit
Of the mercenary planting a flag
Next to the wall where his bookcase stood,
The remnants padded out his old army
Rucksack, kept only for the ricochets.

He counted potholes and pavement cracks
As he tumbled down the steep spiral streets,
He listened to dancers, and stood in line
To sweep away another slice of time.
He was afraid – of the cruelest season,
Of the phantom gnawing at his bones
Until they bled, of the chattering masses
And the tactile silence of the darkness.

Third column down in a square inch of print,
Filler beside yesterday's results,
I shivered as the writer typed the words.
The violets and ambers were shedding
Their summer season opposite the bench
Where we plotted and mapped our young lives.
The chill came not only from the autumn breeze –
That brought the ashes of my shattered promise.

After The Years

You were my daring adventure
When youth was almost everything,
When I was open to capture
Like a child's kite loose in a storm –
That roughly spiced steaming city
Seemed to create a kind of worship.

The destructive kind. Where reason
Still existed but could not escape
From the fortified prison
It had built for the affair,
I was ready – to confront the looks
And the cold warnings to beware.

We each smelt of different lives
But you told me you longed to put
Your hands in the fire of being alive,
Really we were like the carefree
Argument of light against the
Ripple of a resting sea.

Now, after the years have melted
To atoms, it is not love but we
Who change, folding the hands we were dealt,
As I search your eyes for the last
Time I see the Roman path you chose
Over a future blown in glass.

Men of Steel

The iron yawn of the hungry grabbers
Scooping orange dust from the tanker's bowels,
Has the certainty of mathematics,
Just one of a thousand ferrous rituals
In my nursery of revolution.

My teachers were heroes with orange bands
And accumulations of instruments;
Their sacrificed memories of knowledge
And greasy sacks of strange accoutrements,
Were prizes to my infant ambition.

Summers meant strange bearded mercenaries
Would tell their dry tales of deserts and dust,
I listened but preferred my own creaking
Inventions with their foundations of rust –
My blood ran the shade of mineral ore.

Youth shielded me from the bludgeoning blasts
That turned my fingers to rotting splinters,
Those winds carried their unrelenting songs
Throughout each cruel sentence of winter,
Perfecting their freezing provocation.

Would I have become a different man,
Without the banter and fabrications
Of those men, who moulded and created
The conditions for my new creation;
And how many more lost boys are in their debt?

Meltdown

Let's melt our gold to forge
A statue to the Gods,
Let's lay oysters on our table
And feast and swill and gorge.
Let's holiday for eternity
And never feel the pain,
Of penury's cold fingers
Or blows of stinging rain.
Let's turn the key to borrow
Currency by the sack,
Let's never feel in want again
Let's never pay it back!

Let's keep our golden secret
Let's hide it from the rest,
Let's write in golden juices
A tribute to our debt.
Let's keep the music playing
Let's suck the wine lake dry,
And if they try to catch us
We'll turn the volume high.
Let us fly towards the sun
Wearing our golden crown,
Let's fly as high as they did
Before we melt and drown.

We can't reverse this magic
Or turn to black from red,
Let's plant another seed today
For the money tree is dead!

Medalling

The wheel of the eye keeps a slow measure
As the hands of the tower count us down,
The City is slowly sculptured to fit
The bold imagination of the wreckers.

The uninvited are swept to stripped outskirts,
As cathedrals grow and taunt like weeds
Strangling wheat in a forgotten field,
Fed by the drench of a sponged currency.

Dwellers driven from the public's gaze
Join the queue to walk through Traitor's Gate,
Their music of anger slowly muffled
By the calm drone of a drilled delivery.

Our elite parade under fresh bunting
As red as our quaint antique boxes
And white as ashes from the ancient torch,
Speaking the hazy language of winners!

My lost Isle; hard-boiled by a furious
Austerity and inch by silent inch
Anaesthetised from spontaneity,
Calculates the opportunity lost.

The spirit of blazing Arcadians
Is shamed by this over-rehearsed madness;
We sit with the starting gun to our heads,
As the hands of the tower count us down.

Fire Night

It could have been a succulent full moon,
As whizzers and rocket shells climbed and smashed
The glassy air, sprinkling shards of light
Like a shower of Spanish deblumes.

The early air already smelt of death,
I felt the nibbling at my fingertips
And attempted resuscitation
With visions of soup and desperate breaths.

I clung to the promise of a pasty
(Or a bag of chips if I could behave!),
As I followed another shell streak
The darkness like a drunken firefly.

I remembered those stories of treason;
Of foundations laid with gunpowder
By tight subterranean terrorists
Who prayed for a worthier season.

As strangers we searched the dying flames
For our forgotten bands of fellowship
Smouldering in that November darkness,
But found instead the people we became.

The Music Room

This room is a rock 'n roll rhapsody,
It will stab with the pulse of invention
And soothe with caresses of melody –
An asylum from participation!
Becoming alive with brave vibrations
Of mislaid notes that left an echoing trail,
Pungent with the scent of creation
To gently imbibe and never exhale.
Explode with twists of imagination,
Spraying the four walls with a legacy
Of the different, not impersonation,
And snap the stem of blunt conformity.
You need no invitation, just desire
For this kingdom of tenderness and fire.

The Darkness in the Wind

The money men have spoilt something precious!
Like plastic surgery after stitches
And the flashing of unblemished smiles
The swaggering blades revolve their riches.

Landscape, like memory should not be lost
In these crushed fields of electricity,
Only the unreasoned could wield the blind
Power, to sacrifice our sky and sea.

Who scattered iron seeds on the ocean's floor
And raked the fertilizer of false science,
That allowed this ferrous flora to grow
And spin with well-intentioned defiance?

Their petals will not fall in autumn,
No ripe acorns to feed or reseed
Unwitting neighbours sharing the grey deep,
Only man could fashion these iron weeds.

Booms and clanks from yesterday's industry
Will compete with a new century's hum;
Rising voices in an argument of
Who we were and could carelessly become.

Not even night draws its blanket over
This neat parade reflecting through the mist;
No-one asked before they stole my horizon,
Before the money men reaped their harvest.

Missing

The crooked table next to the window
With the view of a sea as turbulent
As our final days, still framed the lukewarm
Brew and half-eaten Eccles cake.

The chatter of office politicos,
The superheated screech of the broken
Cappuccino maker, could not submerge
The silence, that accidental silence.

I nattered about my stirring morning,
About the letter that would change our lives.
Days, the long month disappeared to somewhere else
As I gently asked you to marry me.

I'd dropped by our dandelion fields
The day before, where you modelled your chains,
Where winds blew silent in morning air
As unpolluted as our first day.

I climbed our honeycomb rock, defiant
As I counted the reverential waves
Surrounding our hiding place. I smiled
And placed my hand in yours as darkness fell.

If I had left the game to catch my train
I would not hear the echoes of laughter,
Or follow shadows in the breeze;
When I reach you would be waiting there.

Winterbourne View

How did they perfect their neglect
And laugh at the peal of alarms,
Of those who earned the right not to raise their voices?

And why were those unled malevolents
Permitted to humiliate,
And herd those lambs towards the abyss?

Must we lobby and legislate
To shake awake the empathy
Existing above and below the veneer?

And will those warders' minds heal as slowly
As the bones of their charges
Or remain as terminal as gangrene?

The crockery was unbreakable
Like the spirit of those who had faith,
Who expected only kindness in return for age.

It was not the carelessness of ignorance,
That misplacing of humanity;
They chose to drop it by the entrance door
To their playground of infamy and shame.

The Return

Should I partake in this life swarming
The station like sap through the viens
Of a leaf, or should I decompose,
Gradually, without any fuss?
I was not as alone in the hours
Before the dawn as now in this sweltering
Congregation. They say city life
Takes your best years; I must make for the coast.

I am sure in another place these are people
Just like me, and possibly you, reduced
To a state less than human by the need
To be somewhere, anywhere but the unpleasant
Present. They wait with strained manners
Then spring and gather as if buying tickets
For the end of the world; everyone
Has a war-worn look, always avoiding.

I hear only conversations between people
I will never meet, grown men desperate
To tell someone they hardly know they still
Exist. Through the window, tantalising
Models of my best years appear before
Gently lapping into the past, save
I should have my fill of comfort
Or gain an appetite for the forgotten.

The lady beside me asks for the time,
I tell her and remember the old joke
About the dentist. I wonder if she'll
Ask what my intentions are? Only
To make a firmer fist than city life,
Would be my reply. The first stop is announced –
But I stay to answer the final question,
Of this, my closing examination.

Senses

You were authentic once, a noun,
Not masquerading or leaving
Only simulated footprints
Across pixilated ghost towns.

We used to natter over tea
And the afternoon specials,
Sometimes lip reading over
The relentless smash of the sea.

Though in silence we could read each sign;
By the brail of our bones
And the raising of our veils
We caught glimpses of the divine.

Now you are a myth, virtual
And lost, stored on a circuit board,
A perfect prisoner, out of sight
And voice to say your last farewell.

I tried to Friend you yesterday,
Punched out the letters of your name
Like a pianist without music,
Waiting for your release someday.

The Gathering Hum

It started with anonymity,
Tiny ubiquitous boxes,
Unnoticed as fire extinguishers
Never unloaded in panic.

Stack upon stack, row after row,
Breeding, multiplying their brood,
Rising floor upon floor, suckling
Their sagging coils of fibre-optics.

Pulsating with a supernatural
Growl, the monster is breathing –
Daring its creators to keep
A leash on this son of Cerberus.

Creeping like a bad attitude,
Sprawling acres teem with these
Organs of innovation,
Pumping the invisible blood of trade.

This new life in The Cloud means
Memories stored in salt mines,
Laying dormant in the monster,
Humming its victory song.

The Last Kiss

The was a chill he did not notice as
Each deliberate step dug its brief mark
Into shivering sand, dark as worked clay,
In the quietly encroaching twilight.

He chose a different kind of silence
As he paced his shingled childhood path,
Past the lone flower flourishing on stony ground
Towards his final spurring of senses.

He was leaving behind the fair and just,
The campaigners and remote volunteers,
And abandoning the City's longing,
With its ravenous hunger of Cronus.

The light from her window drew his aching
Limbs towards the cottage like the quiet
Penelope, who hauled her warrior
Through the depths of the gods' conspiracies.

Just once more before the mud-strewn chaos,
Before faith is placed in the world of men
With maps and insignias, armed with their
Lusting instructions from the Stranger's Bar.

He held her innocence in bloodless hands
And gently whispered their northern future,
Consuming her pure energy before,
The masons carved their last memorial.

Blink

The faint whispers of history
In the ears of the grand misled,
Are rising to roars in your kingdom
To awaken slumbering heads.

Do we lack a cornflower sky
Or the boldness to reject?
Will the long beguiled return one day
To restore our right to elect?

Do you have an attribute of God
To justify this divinity?
Please Ma'am place your crown in the ring
Alongside your frayed majority.

I am a captured argon atom
Manoeuvring for liberation,
I am the eyes on your cities' streets
Witnessing the deprivation.

I want to feel the shatter and shake!
To rattle The Castle's gates.
To climb Mr. Brock's monument
And have a hand in the world we create.

The chance to be citizens not
Subjects, to reject this inheritance –
A disorder of a thousand years –
And sever the cord without vengeance!

How dare we pose on our lectern
To scorch the earth with doublethink,
Please Ma'am place your crown in the ring,
Revolution rumbles in a blink.

Your Usual Place

You were missing from your usual place,
But still, I paid the stranger for my tea
And sat in my sun whitened window seat,
Trying to find you in the crowd outside.

I dreamt of a year in that single hour,
Feeling the raw darkness of December;
I counted down the slow tocks of Spring,
As the clock crept around without mercy.

Perhaps you were a customer that day,
Enjoying the novelty of service,
But the machines had different movements
And beat another tune that afternoon.

The laughter and chatter were deafening,
The players familiar with their lines,
I tried to lip-read their plans and secrets,
Hoping to catch a whisper of your name.

Shadows flew by like flies in summer heat,
Each one had possibilities of you,
But I knew before I opened my eyes,
You would be missing from your usual place.

In Defence of a Free Press

Without its fire we are nothing,
If doused we cease to exist,
We should not blunt the probing thorns
Of uncorrupted journalists.

Who allowed this legislation
To be drafted on a whim,
And what other grave agendas
Are crafted by the victims?

Let's daub the colours of freedom,
On liberty's predators,
Never to dwell in a darkness,
Painted by weak amateurs.

Our duty is to satirize
With bravery and confidence,
Retaliating with free speech,
Not scheming in the silence.

We cannot share their ignorance,
Or dismiss Magna Carta,
Why did they bargain our free press
To the binds of Royal Charter?

Those golden boys should hang their heads,
For this myopic judgment,
Shattering our right to reply –
Who will write our First Amendment?

Ignite the beacon and believe,
That freedom is not beyond rescue,
After the gamble of our silver,
For the vanity of the few.

Butchering

It's the sharpening I remember most,
The whoosh and clack of knife on abrasive,
As I craned to marvel at the method
Of the man I imagined in battle,
Parading and slicing like a Viking
Granting no quarter to a new conquest,
To the line of Thursday regulars.

The air was full of strange fractions and cuts,
Halves of best brisket, quarter pots of brawn
Passed over glass into arm locked handbags,
I thought about Abraham as cleavers
Cracked against their ruby-red alter wood,
I squeezed Mam's hand as the whispered
Words were passed that made our Sunday joint.

Now the banter and blood play no further
Part as I ponder the anonymous
Rows of cellophane. The paint now bubbles
And flakes like Sunday's crackling, each side
Of The Square shuttered and boarded and smeared
With the consequences of apathy –
Skewered by a sharper coldblooded blade.

Birth

Each inflicted birth of community
Bring labour pains of upheaval and hurt,
The cornerstone of tradition crumbles,
Into mountains of rubble and dirt.

Revolving towers stretch their grey sinews,
Dumping, and hoisting each skeletal shell,
Laying foundations for a scared new world,
Etching a book of new stories to tell.

Dogs' complaints and children's whimpers carry
The dust ridden air like artillery,
Shaking awake comatose passions;
Reuniting the scattered family.

The rattle of pneumatic percussion
Is the soundtrack to this exhibition,
As the cold Westminster breeze blows a kiss,
From this unmerciful coalition.

As we submit to the arrow of time,
And endure our slow ascent,
Let us stride towards the kingdom
To await our final judgment.

We are the hydrogen and the helium,
The atoms of our constellation,
So let's nurture our newborn neighbourhoods,
Before we say our last Amen.

Breathe

I am forever asking for the time,
Wanting to capture it in a bottle,
Ram home the cork, place it on the top shelf,
Then ignore it while I take a breath,
It makes no sense when loose and free to roam,
Unseen, making us late and ending our days.

I must have the look of a prisoner,
Unable to either tolerate or
Embrace his jailer as I meander
Through the ticking performance of routine,
I rub shoulders with objects, those that have
Seen it all, that wait with stubborn patience.

I talk to Coleport Ladies of Fashion,
The cornered writing desk that outlived
Tyrants and wears the scars from acid tears,
I talk to the oak on my long morning
Walk to the station, I ask how many
Echoes are buried in each faithful ring.

Inside, a thousand synapses collide
In their evolving carnival chaos,
While our celestial neighbours silently
Revolve in their clockwork ceremony;
To understand is to submit, that is why,
I am forever asking for the time.

Birthright

Can you forgive us? The chaos
We have executed was just
For you. When plucked from the hothouse
Harvest you will find no stardust
Or the brimming cup of optimists.

There will be nothing left but to grieve
For the passing of activity;
Were we so knowingly naïve
To inject without a remedy
And spin a shroud of ivory lies?

We have meddled with Arabia,
And concealed our fearless
Messengers with myopia,
Like the slow crushing madness
Of a decomposing harvest.

You won't receive an invitation
To this improvised tragedy,
To purge the contamination,
Or exorcise the apathy
Of your drunken conductors.

Can you forgive us? We will make
You stand with your back to mankind
Unless you shake yourselves awake,
And drown our orators to find –
Waiting in this wreckage is love.

Christmas Eve

Under a strobe stained sky,
Heavy laden strangers
Bump and slide
Like storm-lashed deckhands.

Stuffed trolleys politely collide,
Silently surging along
Aisles of wonder,
Assembled in September.

The sea reaches high-tide,
Lapping island pyramids
Neatly stacked with idols,
Spying their next wreck.

Inexhaustible breeze blocks
Of spirits and pale ales,
Distract their prey,
Singing their Siren songs.

An aroma of panic
Cuts the reprocessed air,
As if the hour had come,
Or the end game had begun.

Tomorrow's dawn will bring,
The exhausted catharsis,
Inviting a unity in hope
For the coming of our King.

The Bell

Halfway again to his Friday gallon,
Flushed from the morning's intestine sermon,
He thumps and flashes an accomplished grin
From a covert tongue long under his skin.
With an artisan's eye he checks the rise
And rest of one more child to be baptized,
One more walk down the long corridor,
His battle long over before his war.

He smiles to anticipate the long ray
Of secret light, shielding from fresh decay,
As eager students tugging at his tail
Are waved behind the frayed velvet veil.
He rises! Immune to chatter and talk
As the bell begins the green mile's lonely walk.
His thinks upon his lonely lost decade –
For tomorrow he confronts the surgeon's blade.

Mourning Bouquets

I was born into the dim light, bearing
A new existence no different
From the last, touching my words once again.
They began arriving before the post,
The rushed driver searched for a tactful
Smile like an ironed-flat salesman, with only
Freshly cut yellow comfort to sell.

I read the typed card and resisted an urge
To pound my outrage – Mam was not John!
I arranged in the anniversary
Vase kept under the sink with the same care
As each Coleport Lady of Fashion
Was replaced after its weekly polish –
I breathed a different spring scent of death.

All the vans were white! An antidote perhaps
To the approaching sea of monochrome.
I heaped the spicy lilies into pyres
On the still dewy morning grass,
Growing and thriving as if the wide world
Still had a voice to tell its futile tale,
On that morning fresh with best intentions.

Rising Underground

Connoisseurs rally with the slide of the bolt,
The players conceal a rare confidence,
This shelter is a broken string before
Our shared communion of substance.

Inside our offbeat palace, cocooned from
The troubled harmony of naked streets,
The whispered tingle of adagio
Electricity hoists me to my feet.

My home brew! Garage fermented for pulse
And passion-waking high ferocious kicks,
Not the safe mechanical afterglow
Of the flat uniform epidemic.

Choruses detonate their shards of glass,
Sprinkling melodies of provocation
To our delirious congregation –
Lighting fuses of the imagination!

Our music has the ruthless beauty of
Loneliness and grief and unrequited
Love, more potent than worn-out opiates,
Bread and oxygen to the devoted.

The Drifter

I did not expect a paying lodger
That paid such close attention to house rules,
There was never a mess or expletive,
No crossed words or fruitless feuding,
Only a dignity in our silence –
I had welcomed a patient listener;
One day I thought I caught a labored breathing
Before noticing the vanishing prey.

I did not foresee explicit beauty
In that perfectly black gangling body,
But no twenty first century device
Could devise such fragile delicacy;
Such a seemingly pointless ambition!
This practiced knitting of snowdrop
Patterns on edges and dark corners –
Perhaps to bequeath a shy legacy?

Had we undergone a separation
That made this a blood-red reunion,
As we rubbed along like vague relations?
Really it was a case of passing through,
Of gaining a measure of each other
Like a pair of unattached networkers,
I wonder now if our friendship endured
In my drifter's careful memory?

Looking Away

It wasn't my fault!
I didn't notice the absence of
Light in her window, or the stuffed
Letterbox dripping onto the bottles
Gathering on the concrete step. I
Was just going around and around
My business, day by day.

When you whispered I knew, like
Some sunken chest had yawned in
The recesses of my mind.
Did those once soft hands and
Manicured nails grasp and scratch
To reach the ringing telephone, or
Slowly unclasp allowing a mug
Of tea to trickle?

I could have asked after
Her niece
Or was it nephew in France?
Or if her strawberries were as
Sweet as last years'.
Now I'll never have the chance.

The Hall

The Hall is a Cello sonata,
The rooms made real with each
Deliberate stroke.
The ladies are long since passed
Into the framed timbers, shoring
Up a skeleton gnawed to splinters by time.

The walls and floors are mottled with
The scent of heroes and their servants
Who shimmied or scurried from
Upstairs to down.
Their souls peel like the ancient plaster
From walls long since left to rot.

Each room is a rising, scaling note.
Every creak of board or gust through
Punctured window
Reaches perfect pitch.

Society

You pay no interest for membership,
No red reminders to paralyse,
No secret black-ball ceremony
Or summons to break out your disguise.

If you raise the back gate to celebrate
The dizzying alchemy of melody,
Down every city street you would hear
The joy and the madness of industry.

The graveled yewk of the everyday gulls,
The flat baritone of the rag and bone,
The stretched rhythm of next door's flapping hinge
Distracts the terror of standing alone.

Do you feel the bare isolation
Of the outcast of the kingdom,
The final pixel in the stadium,
After the rage of the ringing anthems?

You pay no interest for membership,
No days of judgment from deities,
If you roll away the stone to inhale
The resurrection of society.

House of Words

From the hub of your smart inventions and
The pinball frenzy of a Saturday,
You may not notice this undefended
Fortress of accumulated knowledge,
Of twists and daydreams from the forgotten,
But if you enter you will smell the deft
Intelligence under supervision
From the inheritors of myths and yarns.

This understanding does not radiate;
Odours of learning cannot penetrate
The pixilated hum of high street air,
It is in the bouquet from curled leather
Jackets, and through still active tremors
Of formidable artisan passions,
That maps can be redrawn and distances
Narrowed for the benefit of the young.

Only through these tactile encounters can
We assemble the jigsaws of knowledge,
Running fingers down brittle jagged spines,
Cradling each key to the next kingdom;
How could such twisting branches of deeply
Buried beauty survive without daily
Interventions of rediscovery?
Could it be that first douse of midnight oil?

The Executioner Was Late

I felt an unexpected draft of sun
Just after the howl at the thirteenth chime,
The studied formalities had begun
As I grieved for the passing of my line.
I sensed the spots of eyes along the Tower –
The vexed snapping of a splintered timepiece,
And silent gathering crowds past the hour
All coveting perhaps my sharp release?
I counted silences between drum beats,
Like the gaps between lightening and thunder,
Hoping Death's loaded dice were ripe to cheat
And land to frustrate the dragging under.
I cradled that sudden reprieve from fate,
Because the Executioner was late.

Nightfall

A flock of starlings swarm in formation,
A pixilated cloud celebrating
Survival and the day's late persistence.
Smoke rises relentlessly from the yard
Of an anonymous book-end terrace,
Towards four men shaking hands on a green,
I wonder which one stole his victory;
Who would muster patience for his story?

Tired clouds spread along the horizon
Turning the shade of aging porcelain,
As the furnace lights begin to flicker
And twinkle like the searching eyes of youth,
A reminder that this belching relic
Still lives, exhaling, banging its slow pulse.
I remember its din and greasy heat
In this stillness of early evening.

Darkness is extinct! The deeper light falls
The brighter we are illuminated,
And the blacker the smoke strolling towards
The town, towards the music of nocturnes
And a different kind of activity.
This must be a night to inhale courage,
To ask her and not chance again to hope,
On this perfect night of stillness and thought.

Sunken Uplands

When long stretched exiles see fit
To abandon their dawn sharpeners,
Hidden by the blue-sky wit
Of decade old campaigners,
They tell their tales of merry days
Spent on verandas, gorging fruit
So ripe they swear you'll be amazed!
Forgetting their frozen terraced roots.

They expect the fevered green-eyed tune
To play, that we'll wish we're maiden kings,
There to share a gin at noon,
Before the aimless wanderings
Down familiar paths not walked since
Yesterday, like a Catalan Sisyphus
Whose lazy labours make me wince
At their counterfeit Olympus.

Like a stubborn Old Bailey witness
Who dare not speak the shameful truth
They cling to their void of excess,
Draining the fountain of youth.
Like addicts in a web half spun,
These exiles would expire without
Their packages from Albion,
Sustaining through their dogged drought.

Give me my drizzled promenades,
My tired end of pier turns,
Give me my bacon and my Bard,
Fish suppers and the sting of Burns.
I'll take my winter and my spring,
My long darkness before the dawn,
Than their idle Spanish fling;
Not lanced by distant debauched thorns!

Lunchtime Drinking

Perched again, he angles the dregs
Of his swift forth or fifth, the men
Who joked about those hollow legs
And a face the colour of grout
Look away, he mumbles the rehearsed
Defence, engineered to end his drought.

His shaking gruel-grey fingers
Point and tap his favourite badge,
And the whisper that he must not linger
Is pushed into his naked room,
As the swift sixth or seventh settles
And parades its black costume.

He knows this belongs to the young
As he nods and pretends to understand,
Asking why he is among
The duty-free and left-alone,
In the middle of an afternoon
He no longer can postpone.

He had placed a mug of steaming tea
By her side, and closed the open
Book left open on her marble knee,
Then turned the dial to five in hope
It was just a long dream,
And not the tearing of the rope.

Released

As Edward hugged his threadbare case,
Relieved to have escaped his rut,
The street betrayed no welcoming
Fizz, as the ancient gates snapped shut.

Iron clouds raked overhead
As Edward tossed his only coin,
And turned to walk the foreign streets,
Of hidden worlds he must rejoin.

He recognized a passer-by
From his time of righteousness,
But dared not raise his arm to call,
For fear of a public justice.

As drizzle turned to sheets of hail,
Edward cursed the brutal skies,
And turned to face his feared refuge –
The old church where he was baptized!

The clergyman began the prayer
(The one he dreaded to recite),
While Edward met the tortured stare
Of a spectre 'neath the blemished light.

The tumbling prayer books broke the calm
Of the unsuspecting flock,
As Edward drained to silhouette
And broke to flee The Devil's Knock!

Candles scattered down the aisle
When, stubborn as the hanging storm
He raced to blot the flash of fear –
Of that terrifying form!

Sleet assaulted horrified eyes
As Edward weaved around the graves,
Until he faced the name he feared,
The nemesis he could not save.

He stopped and gulped the sodden air
As heavy as his failed conscience,
And read the dedications to
The victim of his night's excess.

Edward cursed that fateful day
Then whispered an oath to confess,
But made to drown the day, before,
A sudden screech announced the darkness!

A circle formed to understand
Edward's failing valediction,
Yet the Spirit only could perceive
His faint request for absolution.

The crowd witnessed the getaway
As the killer sidestepped arrest,
While the watching apparition was
Released at last to find her rest.

The Cleveland Bay Charger

When Daphne slurped the early morning mist
And withdrew to shed the night's excess,
She chose an unfamiliar way
Not contemplating a long return;
The unfolding sunrise broke the brittle sky
Like the slow recall of a buried prayer.

Daphne envied the dreams of sleeping birds
As she surfaced to a ragged thick-set field,
Where in the centre stood a shapeless sight,
A faded beggarly conformation –
A matted spit of equine form
Betraying no shadow in the kindling light.

As she drew the mane from lifeless eyes,
And asked how could the world reject
And overlook, a voice engaged
To ask how could this girl simply stumble
Upon a sight discovered by no other,
From age to long isolated age.

Daphne pondered how the varnish
Of an earlier grandeur could be turned
Like the darkening of a summer's sky,
When the voice confessed its distant act
Of slaying a man through the storm of madness
Across a narrow sea, on fields seeded with lies.

The sun had not reached the peaceful tree
Tips as Daphne dashed to catch her train,
And vowed one question on her planned return
To that place existing in her dreams;
What story lay beyond the knotted coat
And ragged mane, one day she would learn.

The clocks refused to chime before the shy sunrise,
Though the field was bare save for a lone foal
Beside a cracked tombstone. Daphne knelt to intone
A final dispatch; from the Royal Scots Greys –
Fell Saving His Master, Brimeaux, Nineteen
Hundred and Eighteen – carved into the yellowing stone.

Contamination

If Rosie had not caught the train
Into the village of her birth,
She may have sewn her lonely grain
And not prayed for her still rebirth.

The bunting flapped upon the green,
The table groaned with pies and flans,
As the opaque limousine
Scattered the royal garrison.

Rosie soon forgot her errand
And morphed into her red disguise,
She gazed the site to eye a friend
To share this unexpected prize.

The crowd was held behind the rope,
But Rosie's hand reached out to take
The Prince's hand, not just in hope,
But certain that she would not wake.

A note was passed amongst the guards
To whisper in those innocent ears,
To begin his loathsome charade
Outside of his feeble veneer.

Rosie soon found herself entombed
Among his withering opulence –
Under gazes of unfeeling heirlooms,
No time left now for defiance!

The Prince warned of the end result
(As talons wrapped her shaking hands),
Of breathing of this vile assault –
A fate no mortal could withstand!

As thoughts dissected what befalled,
Just one relinquished tear fell,
And to the object of her gall
Rosie mapped her cool reprisal.

Though the stripped streets gave no refuge
And thoughts refused to lay dormant,
All was despair with naught to lose –
Until the Situations Vacant!

So the masquerade began,
Then as days stretched with numb activity,
Rosie resolved without regret,
To douse his mug with mercury!

As the radiant dawn arose,
She glided like divine Thetis,
Contented with the plan she chose –
Down the pathway of catharsis.

As national mourning was declared,
The state threw all its desperate dice,
The Avenger (though warned to beware)
Slept peacefully in paradise.

The Pear Tree

The harvest hangs like an organized
Suicide, stretching its body's
Elastic limbs to submission.
Not ripe, not yet, not until the
First fraying of wind fatigued stalks
And the provocation of the lone fruit's
Bass thump makes its indelible mark.

Is this the first beat of the drum
That plays on the border between
Maturity and slow decay?
Or the first patient footmark
Of a new birth, sneaking in an
Extra season like a First
Footer, glad to take a second chance?

The Prize

The conspirators remain in the shade
Alongside the cunning nominators,
Each New Year and grand anniversary
The chosen and entitled come.

Rogue whispers spread before the lists are drawn
By relentless unbending panjandrums,
Who memorize a constitution that
Humiliates our numb Fount of Honour.

This unconscious deference allows
One lacerating lap or vault,
To sew the ribbons of Empire orders
To a Technicolor coat of glory.

The roll-call of distain does not alter
In this ceremony of acceptance,
As familiar as the rolling tide of grief
For another lost English summer.

The audacity of this rank honour!
The word is honeycombed – as riddled
As the men who peddle them at market
In their chequebook á la carte auction.

I hail the invisible millions!
The carers and children of fortitude,
Our fury could shake the sword from its sheath
If we only march our steps in unison.

Arcade Murder

One flash of unpolluted teeth
Cannot begin to betray,
The next line on their agenda,
The targets for dispatch today.

Like teens in a seaside arcade
Pumping their coins as a dare,
Their victims are nothing but pixels,
Collateral in cross-hairs.

From stations in Arlington County,
Where a satellite reflection
Undergoes interrogation,
With a dumb justification –

The solitary hums are hurled
For the hunt to the unmapped
Caves and forgotten valleys,
To launch their bile-yellow trap!

Like the long faded echo
Of a primeval curse,
The screams do not breach the borders
Of their underground universe.

They turn their eyes from the rising
Smoke and parades of the dead,
To red blips on the killing screen –
Unforeseen tears never shed.

This next seductive slip along
War's rancid evolution,
Will wash remorse from the bloody hands
Of this, their clinical solution.

Hope It Rains

Have I become an exhibit,
A curio without an
Audience to entertain?
When did time cease to have less
To with stretching hours,
Than the gaps between the rain?

I am certain I accumulate
A denser layer of dust
Than my patient performers,
Perhaps it is insulation –
A defence donated by the dead
To lock in the punch of sulphur?

These could be the times these models
Had lives, not just the frozen
Features of those who had outraged
The Gods, I only guess at the
Fashions by those who step carelessly
Onto our deadpan stage.

Am I now one of the family?
Their idiosyncrasies are as
Familiar as the damp cracks
And oxygen fueling the candles
Of time, quietly dissolving
My forgotten House of Wax.

Wake

Routine is the best they say,
So I become the sole player
Of my own dark performance and lay
Under the carefully folded layers,
As the mayhem of the waking hour,
Falls silent, giving no excuse
Not to be consumed by the potent power
Of the night to comfort and seduce.
But when the shadowy seductions fail
Time lingers heavy on the breath,
And trying comes to no avail
When it is easier to imagine death.
But I push on through and stare
Into the yellow mottles circling above,
And count the humans who would care
Or feign to testify their love.
If my efforts fail and brightness fades
The unconscious land would pass by, yet
To wake would be to step from shade,
And remember hope and not forget.

The Saltscar Osprey

What shift in fields sent you soaring
Short of December's African climes?
You, the image of Theseus
Born free from the shackles of land,
To arc and glide halfway beyond
Your kingdom's silent radius.

Was I a grain in your long sweep?
A new audience for golden
Eyes beneath your dark disguise?
You made your nest amongst nets
Nibbled by time's hostile claws,
Your *yewk* prompting the shy sunrise.

I was an overwhelmed student
Of your cool sedation, seeking
Your mottled breast's rise and fall
As your frigid eyes guarded
Us both each passing day, through
The hushed waters before the squall.

Afterwards, I surfaced to hear
Only a lapping swell and distant
Hysteria. The sunrise was late
As I scoured the waking sky
To tell you how you saved my life;
You, my warrior at the gate.

Switch Off The Light

I unplug myself and switch off the light
At this fertile hour of a lost night,
And close my eyes so I can see you.

Can we all remember the sensation
Of daring to love, and gulping the thrill
Of receiving that love in return,
Like a draft of sun on a winter's day?

My memories were once as merciless
As hailstorms, to close my eyes would be
To hear the choking music of desire.

But only dreams now possess the power
To release that raw electricity –
I can wake with the sweat of my first kiss
Filling my eyes with the sting of elation.

I could not abide the bare knuckle and
Bone of naked truth, without the soft flesh
Of sensation, plugging the gaps with
Fictions of the imagination.

I wait for the darkest hour of night
So I can lose myself in you until,
I switch on the light and open my eyes.

The March

It was a party of misunderstandings,
Invites opened by the unintended.
Disparate, desperate angry wanderers,
Shot glasses of sweet and sour liquors
Poured into a thin fragile glass.

Miss-spelt slogans seemed to hover,
As the paint dripped like the end credits
Of a budget horror, then thrusted in
Tune to the improvised chants and
Piercing yells.

A join-the-dots line of glossy
Yellow at our east and west
Kettled our ranks into neat little rows.
Some laughed, encouraged.

Others were so still, so solemn,
Movement would have been as
Shocking as the South Bank statues.
Some had forgotten why, others
Hopped into the warmest bed;
So easily led.

The generals glimpsed our destination
As waves of cheers undulated through
Our insubordinate ranks. Artillerymen
Discharged volleys of invectives before
A mounted dot launched an electronic
Counter in a language lost on everyone.

Suddenly we halted, exhaling like a
Tired accordion short of a note,
Craning for the next act.